Ancestry

Ancestry Scrapbook

Ancestry Scrapbook

Ancestry Scrapbook

Ancestry Scrapbook

Ancestry Scrapbook

Ancestry Scrapbook

Ancestry Scrapbook

Ancestry Scrapbook

Ancestry Scrapbook

Ancestry Scrapbook

Ancestry Scrapbook

Ancestry Scrapbook

Ancestry Scrapbook

Ancestry Scrapbook

Ancestry Scrapbook

Ancestry Scrapbook

Ancestry Scrapbook

Ancestry Scrapbook

Ancestry Scrapbook

Ancestry Scrapbook

Ancestry Scrapbook

Ancestry Scrapbook

Ancestry Scrapbook

Ancestry Scrapbook

Ancestry Scrapbook

Ancestry Scrapbook

Ancestry Scrapbook

Ancestry Scrapbook

Ancestry Scrapbook

Ancestry Scrapbook

Ancestry Scrapbook

Ancestry Scrapbook

Ancestry Scrapbook

Ancestry Scrapbook

Ancestry Scrapbook

Ancestry Scrapbook

Ancestry Scrapbook

Ancestry Scrapbook

Ancestry Scrapbook

Ancestry Scrapbook

Ancestry Scrapbook

Ancestry Scrapbook

Ancestry Scrapbook

Ancestry Scrapbook

Ancestry Scrapbook

Ancestry Scrapbook

Ancestry Scrapbook

Ancestry Scrapbook

Ancestry Scrapbook

Ancestry Scrapbook

Ancestry Scrapbook

Ancestry Scrapbook

Ancestry Scrapbook

Ancestry Scrapbook

Ancestry Scrapbook

Ancestry Scrapbook

Ancestry Scrapbook

Ancestry Scrapbook

Ancestry Scrapbook

Ancestry Scrapbook

Ancestry Scrapbook

Ancestry Scrapbook

Ancestry Scrapbook

Ancestry Scrapbook

Ancestry Scrapbook

Ancestry Scrapbook

Ancestry Scrapbook

Ancestry Scrapbook

Ancestry Scrapbook

Ancestry Scrapbook

Ancestry Scrapbook

Ancestry Scrapbook

Ancestry Scrapbook

Ancestry Scrapbook

Ancestry Scrapbook

Ancestry Scrapbook

Ancestry Scrapbook

Ancestry Scrapbook

Ancestry Scrapbook

Ancestry Scrapbook

Ancestry Scrapbook

Ancestry Scrapbook

Ancestry Scrapbook

Ancestry Scrapbook

Ancestry Scrapbook

Ancestry Scrapbook

Ancestry Scrapbook

Ancestry Scrapbook

Ancestry Scrapbook

Ancestry Scrapbook

Ancestry Scrapbook

Ancestry Scrapbook

Ancestry Scrapbook

Ancestry Scrapbook

Ancestry Scrapbook

Ancestry Scrapbook

Ancestry Scrapbook

Ancestry Scrapbook

Ancestry Scrapbook

Ancestry Scrapbook

Ancestry Scrapbook

Made in the USA
Las Vegas, NV
15 October 2023

79125648R00059